Four Swedish Poets

Four Swedish Poets

Lennart Sjögren
Eva Ström
Kjell Espmark
Tomas Tranströmer

Translated by Robin Fulton

White Pine Press

Translations © 1990 Robin Fulton
Original work copyright by authors
ISBN 0-934834-97-0

Publication of this book was made possible, in part, by grants from The National Endowment for the Arts, The New York State Council on the Arts, and The Swedish Institute.

Acknowledgements

Most of the translations in this book have already appeared in various magazines and acknowledgements are due as follows:

Kjell Espmark: *Cave* (New Zealand), *The Hudson Review* (N.Y.), *Inside Sweden* (Stockholm), *The International Portland Review* (Oregon), *Ninth Decade* (London), *Oasis Books* (London), *Shearsman* (Malaysia), *Swedish Books* (Gothenburg), *2PLUS2* (Lausanne).

Lennart Sjögren: *Inside Sweden* (Stockholm), *Ninth Decade* (London), *Verse* (Oxford).

Eva Ström: *Frank* (Paris), *Inside Sweden* (Stockholm), *The Poetry Review* (London), *2PLUS2* (Lausanne).

Tomas Tranströmer: *Inside Sweden* (Stockholm), *Poetry Wales* (Mid Glamorgan), *Swedish Book Review* (Lampeter), *2PLUS2* (Lausanne), *Verse* (Oxford).

The translator would also like to thank the poets themselves for their helpful cooperation.

White Pine Press
76 Center Street
Fredonia, N.Y. 14063

Contents

Contents

Contents

Contents

Translator's Preface

In the introduction to his splendid versions of Paul Celan's poems (Anvil Press Poetry, London, 1988) Michael Hamburger uses a phrase which to me seems an accurate description of how the translator of poetry has to wait and listen for the right moment. "It was a question not of whether I could catch this allusion or that..." he writes, "but whether I could respond to the gesture of the poem as a whole. If the gesture of the poem came home to me, the oddities of diction and usage, including the ambiguities, could usually be conveyed in English..."

This "gesture of the poem as a whole" has a lot to do with the poem's own native language, obviously enough, with what Frost called "something in the way the words are curved and all that—the way the words are taken, the way you take the words." Those words are from Frost's interview with Cleanth Brooks in 1959, and they follow immediately upon a statement which has often been wrenched out of context and given a dogmatic certainty it was never meant to carry—"I like to say, guardedly, that I could define poetry this way: It is that which is lost out of both prose and verse in translation." He was talking "guardedly," tentatively, in a specific context.

For "the gesture of the poem as a whole" is more than the words on the page or the voice in the air: its origin is the imagination which marks the page or disturbs the air. Our response to the gesture, as reader or interpreter or translator or as all three, is as much a question of tuning in to a particular imagination as to a form of words. True, we start with words on a page in one language, and we finish with words on a page in the other language, but in the space between, I'm sure, something mysterious and nonwordy happens.

My justification for choosing these four Swedish poets, and not another four, is simply that all four have produced "gestures" to which as a translator I have found myself responding. I would not say that they are "the best four" or "the most representative" for statements like that would lead us into critical language which I don't care for. I would say, though, that they are undoubtedly among the most interesting poets writing in Sweden today.

Tomas Tranströmer is already well-known to English language readers and all of his published poetry up to 1986 is available in English, many poems in differing versions by different translators. He is therefore represented here by a group of poems written and published very recently.

1

The other three poets, Kjell Espmark, Lennart Sjögren and Eva Ström are represented by poems written over a fuller period of their writing lives. They are not yet well known outside Sweden but I think they deserve to be so, even if through the distoring clarity of another language.

—Robin Fulton

Four Swedish Poets

Lennart Sjögren

The Barn

Through the crack in the wall they saw a dead person. The barn was high, it smelled faintly of last year's hay, in the morning the light fell in clearly. There was in fact only the one crack in the tightly-made wall where it was possible to peep through. A knot which had worked itself out of the edge of the plank widened the crack significantly. They were drawn there, looked in, looked at each other: there she lay. Two trestles, a sofa-lid, a white sheet, and the profile which was now so firm and uplifted. But the eyelids lay deep.

They looked at her and remembered her like this for the rest of their lives. When the one of them died, more than seventy years later, the other, the survivor, found himself thinking first of all not about the man who had just died but about the woman who lay straight and white in the clear morning inside the barn. And he saw her face.

Lennart Sjögren

The Forests

And further and further away in the forest. Further and further in, where the blood-red cocks crow. Where paths, bewilderingly alike, at last give out. The pathless takes over.

In there, where fragments of crashed planes lie and no-one comes searching for them. A locomotive stands wedged between a time that is abandoned and a time that has not yet come.

In a landscape where seeking does not exist, but where surprise—the kind of surprise which merely surprises, doesn't transform—has opened its diary, covered with unreadable signs. The trees observe one another; on a summer night a stone talks to another stone. The birds of prey that hover motionless on thermals, the doves that fall in abrupt curves as if full of shot, beat their wings. They rise.

No-one recalls anything, morning and evening the faces turn towards and away from each other but without the least indication of a ceremonial act. The forest is crunching. Those on the ground, those in the winds and those in the passageways under the earth are gnawing each other.

8

Clay

Beasts of clay. Birds of salt. Humans of iron. They survive by eating chalk, magnesium, phosphorous, earth. Some gather riches and glitter for a while. Those who seek another satisfaction than that which the minerals can give, don't survive.

Such big birds of salt. With their hard salt beaks they crush the stones and look for the secret substance that could fertilize their eggs. The cocks are sterile and the nests overgrown by the sharp-edged moss that flourishes in salty earth. Likewise, the humans.

The clay beasts listen with tensed ears, those with horns pierce the sky with them, those with pads raise one paw, ready to hop. The humans pick at the earth with spoons, looking for something to eat, hollowing out each other's cheeks.

The Weight

Today, one day in the heat of summer, he is standing straight-backed and straddle-legged. He bears the weight of the sun over his shoulders like a sack of heavy flour. His legs are rooted firmly in the earth.

That the tiny creatures, those who eat their way through the years and transform the big trees to ruins, are advancing through him as well, groping along his arteries and approaching his brain—he doesn't know. No-one knows. No more than the big twin-boled elm knows that years will come when the roots are dead and only the storm to come will give it a deadline.

Yet perhaps he does know. Perhaps that is why he is sweating beneath the weight of the sun.

from Forest Elegies

§§§

If someone now checks the wind in flight
and a bird steps out of the air

say then that a new time has started.

And if the trees when they listen
leave their roots
and move towards the morning to drink
then
quite a new season has begun.

§§§

The weight now falling over the landscape
and the lips
the clouds open over those
who for so long have been without water.
All those now going there
to meet, at last, rain.

When the leaves in their arteries
see how lakes appear
and those stones
which for so long have been covered with silence
can again be heard speaking.

§§§

Rose at four one summer morning
watched by a weasel
and further off in the cold
a crow.
Burned books
also old worn-out clothes.

Thought then hope existed
soon gave up that idea.

Put out a boat on the lake
there saw a hand. An oar.
Heard footsteps that came towards me then left.
Heard the oar.

§§§

A tree which is someone's pyre
and the pyre which is a mouth
the tongue which rises here and wants to speak about
what can't be spoken about:

I the tree
I the living-to-the-last
I have formed the wings
so that they visit me
I have asked the water to step in
so that we can converse.
I held
a cuckoo's head in my arms
he crowed when morning came.

Last night lightning visited me
he split me
but my life and the lightning's make the nights
luminous.

I leaned over someone's inconsolable grief
she said she was dead
I let her drink out of me
until she was no longer thirsty

Early One Summer Night

Creation winks
the nightjar minds his business
the hay dries
and the cuckoo just laughs
it lays its egg and laughs.

Lennart Sjögren

from Beasts

The ant-heaps furthest in
where all paths peter out.
Other creatures than men
live there
but like men they gather fuel.

And they get the better of deepest winters
in another deep.

Ice

Such as had an interest
in selling ice
once gathered on the lakes
with long saws.

Then when the day was very still
it could be heard to death's kingdom
how chunks were sliced from winter's flesh
and the fishes saw a well in the sun.

The Bird

There are south-facing studios
windows covered with thin wax-paper
in them are easels
and an abandoned dried bird.

Then there are attics in deserted farmsteads
with the same silence:
rake-teeth high as fingers
but no more summers are raked through them.

And then at last there is the heart
where the dried bird
itself built its dead nest.

The Thresholds

His house he's leaving now
abandoning what's clear-to-see
and asks for time to-think-about-it.

A shining in the jaws, in the skeleton.

Paws, bird-eyes
so raised, lucid
and the altogether astonishing feathers.

Altogether taken-by-surprise
with a somewhat stiff smile
he thus abandons the thresholds.

Afterwards

One day long afterwards
someone lays a hand on the scarred skin:
"It doesn't still hurt?"
"No, it doesn't hurt."
"Touching doesn't hurt?"
"Touching isn't felt."

But the one who asks and the one who answers
know
that day is already late
and answer and question
now mean something else.

City Image

I saw a pike's head
rise above the square
I saw a big goose, it was taller
than the town hall
and more powerful.
I a visitor
in the world's smaller cities
felt my skin creep
when the pike spoke of sorrow
and of the indescribable joy
when she ate of the grass
at the river's edge.

Heard

Heard in the middle of the night
in the winter night
how birds sang

from other seasons

but it was not the lark
and not the icy swan.

After Sleep

He falls asleep in the afternoon. Meanwhile the clouds rise. When he wakens summer is past. The heat which made the grass wither and the wells dry up is past. The sky which was so blinding is past.

He goes out in the forest to see if the water-hole still holds water. He has been sleeping for only half an hour. The cows stand black beneath the foliage, they look hard at him. Can it really be that they know an age has vanished since the morning, is he a stranger to them, someone they would no longer acknowledge?

The metal of the car body is now harder and more silent than before, the faces mirrored in it are closed. And the house-roofs, whether tin or tile, have stored up within themselves an absence which makes the tongue dry.

Yet no great thunderstorm has drawn past. Only a cloud-back. It has given neither rain nor lightning. But the sleep came and worked a change. Out of the sea the fish call to him to come down there.

Everything is fin-like, before the age of man.

Lennart Sjögren

The Snails

In early autumn
when the brief age of the snails
is at last here
they take themselves out along the roads.

They stretch out their feelers
to see
where death has his hut.

The Oar

Anyone finding a smashed oar
can't with certainty say
a shipwreck has happened

but it is likely a rower
has been on the water

a forgetfulness may have risen in him
his name
he abandoned to the current
and renounced the possibilities of the oar.

The Wallpaper

The birds play in the wallpaper
and while the early morning light
makes its way through the window
and before
anyone has wakened
and when those who have kept watch
have at last fallen asleep
the dying man rises in his bed
and the birds lift from the wallpaper.

The Mountain

There are no mountains here
the wading-birds walk about in low water
they pull worms out of the sand
and swallow.

Anyone who wants mountains
will have to build them in his soul.

Who Doesn't Dream

I saw a rat come across the road
she had a human face
she was a little rat
smaller than my shoe.
She asked which way to turn
to find where she could die in peace.
How could I answer such a question
which was so like my own.
I tried with something half-biblical:
go to the place where the dead bury
their dead—perhaps it is in the west.
That didn't help
and when I changed it to:
go to the place where the unborn
meet those still living—perhaps it is in the east,
and ask if a reasonably priced death
can be obtained there
she'd already gone.

And who doesn't dream of a quiet death
—the sooner the better one says
without meaning what one says.
If it were frosty that day
or summer—I don't remember
but the dreams stood in queues along the road
not unlike birds set up without wings.

In the Month of May

Today as I write you I don't
want to talk either about death
or about the plagues life brings.
I want only
to write about the wind
when it passes through the birchtops
and the light which is now so splendidly
scattered down among the trunks.

It is May.

Perhaps it is possible without guile
at least once in a lifetime
to write like this—
the wind asked me to do so
that wanderer
who is always crossing the frontiers
of the possible.

In the waken dream
the one
when at highest midday
I saw a flock of beasts
grazing by that frontier
the one side was in shadow
the other was blinded by light,
when they turned
light and shadow changed places.

At the time I was hardly surprised
but afterwards
I was surprised
that I had never before seen
such grazing flocks
by such a frontier.

The Snow-Fall

Don't ask me how the blood quietens
in invisible wounds

and don't ask me where the fatherland
still worth defending lies

but ask me rather
about the gathering snow-fall

we can meet and talk about
how what is without hope
has its own hope

and about how those long anxious
over death
are caught by cheerfulness when the snow falls.

Trinity

One trinity I believed in:
the unborn, the living, the dead.

I said
ask the cuckoo about the unborn,
but
she only looked hysterically in her numbered days
for another nest to put her egg.

I said
ask the crow about the living,
but
she was already hunting ravenously
for another carrion scrap.

I said
ask the stone about the dead,
but
it was only listening absently to the cracks
inside itself.

This Calm

Out of what hollow
does this strange calm well up
the marsh replies only with its endless nodding
to every question
and the suburbs
where tonight has seen another murder
show themselves quite absent
they turn away in mist
before a January dawn.

And he who lost the gift of speech
and whose left arm is slack
is standing by the window
drawing in the frosty pane.

If birds would now scratch with their claws
on the same window
and someone take his left arm
in a greeting
he would carry on drawing his signs
which are a conversation
to the side of the tongue
and audible only to the frost
which can read the thoughts of the speechless.

He's been standing there for half the night.

To a Bat

Bat—
I want to praise you for your beauty
now when you've been deprived of your feathers
which also looked like dark fur
and you show yourself here
in your white skeleton.

Why you died I don't know
—perhaps so that my wan days
would at last attain some order
in the face of death and the harder life.

How quiet the winter nights were
when you hung upside-down
enclosed in a heavier sleep than ours
dead you were not
although you looked dead
and a skeleton you are not
although you now look
like a skeleton.
You should be nominated Winter's Angel
—although what title I give you
you'd hardly care.

You were among the fliers
but changed your beak for a rodent's muzzle
you were a little rat with wings.
No doubt you also looked like us
only you had older eyes.

Of course I've wondered how
the flies taste on your palate
on a summer evening
and what you know about the longest night.

The Roses

The phones ring in the empty house, both upstairs and down. The carpets hear them ringing, so do the windows, and the faces inside the picture-frames. But these are all fixed in their places. They trust in Silence to hurry to the phone. The wallpaper roses are imprisoned in the walls and the cutlery is lying, in spite of its sheen, piled together in their compartments like life-time prisoners.

Silence leaps up from his chair, reaches the phone at the third ring, lifts the receiver and replies. But whoever is ringing hears nothing and calls hello in vain.

"It's about someone who's bleeding to death. Answer, for God's sake! Answer, and prevent a tragedy!"

"It's about the sharing out of an inheritance, it's a family matter. You must answer, your silence could have unforeseeable legal consequences."

"It's about someone who's just been born. About the umbilical cord, you must realize!"

"It's about an impending accident which only your voice can prevent. A fateful mistake. Aren't you listening, you must listen!"

Again and again Silence calls out his reply into the receiver. But his voice cannot be transmitted through such wires.

"It's about some flowers that were ordered. Can the roses be delivered?"

But no matter how often the phone rings, nothing helps. The pictures persist with their wailing, and the window-panes still dream of being able to burst free. Silence sits in his chair paralyzed.

The unstopped bleeding proves fatal. The misunderstandings multiply. The umbilical cord is not cut. The inheritance goes to the wrong person. And the roses are left without a recipient.

The Boat

At 8:35 in the evening he drops the anchor. The wind is strong and the boat is already drifting in a dangerous direction. But when he tries to secure the hawser he fumbles in the motion of the rising sea and is quickly driven away from what was his lifeline. He knows already that his last attempt to start the engine will be another failure.

At 9 o'clock the boat touches land. Rudderless and swaying, it has been hurrying towards the rocks and raised by a high wave it heaves up against the shore as if with one exhausting plunge it would reach firm ground and shelter there from the storm. In the calm between two breakers the man jumps overboard. Luck is with him, he finds his footing and saves his life. The boat is pulled out and pushed in again. The wind won't let go: the boat is on a leash and freedom is an optical illusion.

As soon as ten past nine, close to the point where the boat first touched land, a plank near the water-line is violently stretched inwards, a distinct crack appears amidships and the hull starts to fill with water. The solitary man makes his way inland to find people. At first he calls, but the wind is too loud. No lights lead him. No houses are yet visible. It's autumn and darkness is falling quickly. He just leaves the boat, he has to.

The storm and the rocks begin their work of grinding down the stranded body. There's still a light in the cabin. A nautical map, the usual telescope, a pair of gloves, and a half-eaten packet of biscuits—that's what one would first see, looking in the window.

At 11 o'clock a big hole suddenly opens underwater. It seems to happen all at once and without difficulty, but behind this event lie two hours of uninterrupted work on the part of the waves. It's the fatal wound, now opened. The various ribs moan and gradually lose control of the lines of the hull. The lead keel comes loose and settles on the sea-bed. The engine leaves its place, it sinks at an angle and drags with it both rudder and propellor-shaft. The shaft bends into an arc. At the same time the light in the cabin goes out.

The lightened hull is now tossed higher by the breakers, seems more agile. Without the balancing weight of the engine and the keel it is now moving even more helplessly and without any rhythm of its own. Shortly after midnight it is split in two. One half is immediately washed in over the rocks, the other is sucked further south by the current and then tossed ashore. During the rest of the night the scattering of all sorts of lighter fragments continues and they are carried so far away that they cause surprise when they are found.

At some time not recorded, searchlights are visible up on the land. By then the storm has slackened. A few silhouettes can be seen moving in the glare in front of the vehicle before it departs. At 6:20 in the morning in the first glimmering of dawn they come back. The man who was ship-wrecked is one of them. He stands looking at what has happened.

The Copper Pot

The copper expands from within. Because of something which does not belong to the pot but which nevertheless exists within her, the sides move. She's heavy, she's made of chased copper. For a long time she has belonged to the order of the unchanging.

Now she is breaking up. The process has been under way for only a short period. It began just an hour ago. It caused dents and bulges, the sides buckled as if a terrible hand was stretching them. She resists but her shape changes more and more. A deep crease appears on one side, the curve threatens to disintegrate. The tin-plated rim twists awry. She gapes, her cry is distorted. A decisive crack develops.

She now looks like those organic creatures who are so violently transfigured when they encounter life's improbabilities that they can no longer be recognized. She has now been stretched to the limit where it is no longer possible to avoid being broken right through. She folds out, falls and becomes a flattened sheet of copper.

The Apples

The apples fall in the night. The trees are still. Deeper into the forest the ferns are still too. The stars stand where they have stood. Those who read signs in the Milky Way are already predicting an even harder winter. The most vigilant on a night like this are the stones, they listen for each apple that falls.

Two dead people who happen to be walking here through the garden on their way down to the lake for their last dip of the season, also stop. Listen.

"What was it I said?" says the one.

"What did I say?" says the other after a pause.

Then each walks on, in his own thoughts. But they could just as well have been living, on such matters neither the night nor the apples see much difference.

Eva Ström

Amber! Amber!

Your friendliness breaks against me, and that too is good
like a rustling wave burning me around the edges,
jelly-fish drawing their way over my arms, that too is good,

to be annihilated a little—
you thought everything should have a name—you were disturbed
by my namelessness—you wanted to give everything erroneous names,
names that existed,

but I want to give new names, baptize again and again. I danced
for you with honey in my hair, weed in my groin, a light dance,
a dance with white breasts

the rustling wave, the sound of butter frying, a sound
beyond compare, like crinkling silk, you do not wait, nothing
waits, with your warm resin you enclose me in a golden
embrace—

amber, amber, I call to you, while I stiffen
more beautiful than a jewel

How Shall I Save You From Drowning?

How shall I save you from drowning?
How shall I escape the man behind me
the man who smiles at me
and wants to show me his new armored car,
he loves it, he holds me around my breasts

Maybe only because I am queen?
I have never known what courtesy is,
the way he holds open each door for me
means I must always enter rooms
first

I love the open plain,
where the enemy is visible. They're coming now in their thousands,
all nameless. I know that somewhere at one time
they have been described—ridiculous right now
to hunt in some library

I seek refuge in the river-edge
They're combing the reed-beds—but don't find me, I
can swim I can flee.
Then I remember who the enemies are.
There's only one question I can put.
—Who is the leader?
The answer is always the same.
—No-one.

Your Thoughts Are Like Warts

Your thoughts are unpleasant, they are like warts, they
always crop up somewhere else and disfigure me,
your thoughts have deep roots and to be rid of them
I must scrape and scrape till I bleed...
where the blood comes out, there am I.

Leave me, I say. You have built a mountain
over your unwieldy childhood. You have forgotten it
                              and the icy coldness
in the smiles of others when you dared to smile.
You were always inching towards the center,
creeping round the walls,
honey from the walls, darkness and honey

I am implacable, that's all.
I'll shut the door to the most handsome rhinoceros
when he comes to me with his blue gaze from the bush
Can't you see it's snowing in my eye? he says
Can't you see that memories from Trias and Jura
are growing on my hooves?

Your thoughts are like warts, like warts
your eyes are like lakes, like lakes.

ho Are My Wound

You who are my wound
and will never come back
and never be born again.

You who were bright as snow
with skin that has lived through all,
you who were born with a wound in your side,
you who resisted narcosis

I sew you together,
Again and again.

You open the wound,
Again and again.

It's you who have the knife you whisper.
You sound desperate.
Your face is made of snow.
Your tears melt-water.
Daffodils and narcissi from such tears.

Can I come into the room you cry.
I say yes.
When you come in you come very slowly
as if you have stopped wishing for anything.

To Murphy or The First Day of a New Religion

When I was saving for a respirator
the days were easy,
light filled the birchwood at the window,
the spruce-trees grew without a flicker
I drank air and the air wanted nothing

From the land of candy-stores I can now report
how the drop bottles shine over the beds
and guide their inhabitants,
how voices and steps wash through hemispheres of the brain
like warm waves

I wanted nothing, everything became still,
I didn't shave my head, had nothing to do penance for
and the food I ate was barely sufficient for growth,
in other forest-lands, in Ceylon or the Amazon,
tranquil people performed similar exercises
for the pulse still beat

Like a butterfly in dark pigment on a skin
or a cave wall,
or the outline of a beast that promised more
than good hunting,
I slowly take shape and stiffen to a sign
the very first in a brand new alphabet.

I Am Steinkind

I am Steinkind in my black dress,
my body is small and hard, it is granite,
I wasn't born, I was chipped from my mother's womb,
chipped, a huge stone
draped in forests, these lakes and coniferous forests
that are Sweden, my caul

I am Steinkind, all that they said they chiselled into me,
my brain is thousands of rune-stones,
my arms are covered with rock-carvings,
rock-carvings I can never shake off,
they taught me everything, chiselled it into me,
their boats they chiselled into my upper arms,
their pictures of animals they chiselled about my breasts

grain-fields, grain-fields they chiselled around my pelvis,
cut it all into me,
heated it hot and drew with chalk,
and so it stays in me, it stays in Steinkind,
and weathers with me, weathers with me into sand.

When I Woke

when I woke in the morning my skeleton had gone soft,
my skull was the only solid thing left, it crowned
my skeleton like a hard poppy-seed head,
its mushy contents floating in their liquid
by my arms and legs and my spine had gone soft
could no longer carry me

I wondered what to do, one should be practical
my children still small as strawberry flowers needed help,
I couldn't take one step, was stuck on the spot,
perhaps I could make wings like Leonardo da Vinci,
he didn't succeed of course, I could always try,
or wings of wax like Icaros,
he fell of course, I could be more careful,
perhaps I would pour into a plaster cradle or steel corset,
or like the adder acquire stiff elastic swaddling clothes
which wouldn't let me walk but at least I could crawl.

The thoughts whirled in my head, one shouldn't despair
I saw a neighbor washing a window in the sun,
she worked so slowly and painstakingly
it was almost like love,
and I thought: all these humdrum things are now beyond me,
spreading a sandwich, opening a door or a window.

But when night spilled over the rim of morning, a membrane broke:
Give me back ordinary things, quite ordinary, now,
give me insignificant things, the least meaningful,
let me walk to the shop and buy bread and milk,
let me pay for them to the girl who is always dreaming,
let me carry them home, let me walk on *that* road,
give me ordinary things, only ordinary things, now!

The Message-Bearer

Why did you give me the green suit?
why did you give me the green bicycle?

if a lover's purpose is to enjoy
what is God's purpose with men?

only green landscapes, yes, I ran across the fields,
I was your message-bearer in the landscape of conventions

your terrible wrath when I refused to carry out your commands
and your great gentleness when you stroked my knee
and bound it, bound it with white linen...

I can endure much for such a wound,
I deliver your crumpled notes with your
darling, darling, darling,
to the dung-scented cowshed

as I run back I hear the shotgun going off,
It's the rooks getting hit, they tumble on the field,
I run like someone who doesn't want to know,
unable to quit my fetching and carrying,
yet still not forced, not forced.

I Stand in the Warmth of a Man's Hand

Snow White:
I stand on the warmth of a man's hand
I stand on the warmth from a man's hand
I stand in the warmth in a man's hand

we talk about Milles and I say,
how could he make that sculpture,
Man in God's hand,
God's hand is cold,
battered by meteors

I stand on the warmth of a man's hand
I lie down and sleep by the fold of the thumb
I amuse him with my tricks and my sorrow
I stand on the warmth from a man's hand
I have a view of the plain,
I lie right at the edge and peep down

at churches, farms, coffins and animals,
the churches show up white, like single teeth in a black palate,
the hard farms,
the inert coffins,
the painted lilies,
the smell of animals

I stand on the warmth of a man's hand
when night comes the warmth streams out into a cold space
I fall asleep with the beating of an artery under my ear,
and feel the hard pelvis through my soft hip

Already a Long Way Off

Already a long way off they knew it was him
they could not avoid him
he shone a lamp before his steps
he resembled nothing they knew of
perhaps a cripple or a defective
or someone who has long been ill
his face was stiff
nothing of the usual moved there
they had no defense against him and his gifts

he wanted always to touch them, to feel their hands
it was no use hiding
he wanted to talk with just them
the grown-ups laughed but not like when they were happy
they laughed always differently

When he went his way it was something over-and-done-with
one closed the door meaningfully,
when spring then came all this was forgotten
but when the snow melted one would again find
the empty plate one had tried to induce him with

The Outer Hebrides

If it's so you're longing to the Outer Hebrides
or some other place
where you face the sea and turn your back on Europe
where the islands are only a thin membrane of rain
if it's so you're longing to these islands
or others of similar insignificance

if it's so you're tired out with writing
reference books
and reading them from A to Z
if you've taken in the knowledge to be had
of the Jarrah forests and of the Druids
from Tantalus to Tatra

and if it's so the azaleas are withering
their swollen pink blossoms already dried and fallen
and nothing left of their hardiness, their kinship
with Ericacae the all-covering heather,
glass-house flower, glass-house flower...

if it's so you feel the break-up breaking
out, like a crack, or just a thought,
if it's so you're longing to be changed
while you journey
as the unripe fruit is changed as it journeys
in the hold, over the seas, under the Southern Cross,
a ship's hide between it and the water

if it's so and no other way
if it's so
you've already switched the lights off in the house
and you're on the way.

The Unblessed

The unblessed broke a day out of the week and tasted it. It was white, indifferent. The edges of the day were riddled with thousands of small worm-holes, only the core was healthy, a hard compressed piece of inaccessible time. Through this time nothing would pass, time wouldn't move but neither would it stand still. Time had become matter and like matter would grow old.

Huge Wings for a Frail Body

When day approached evening the dusk gathered round a pink doll's
pram that stood parked among the columbines. The grass was high and
the nightingale beat with his dull hard drills against the dense thicket.
The child who had played with the doll's pram had grown up, it hadn't
been able to see the open view or the dark one, the dead earth full of
twigs and waste. What did it resemble? Huge wings for a frail body.

The Mountain-Pass

This mountain-pass on the way to Akra, this road that lost itself... On the few occasions when they had to talk about it, people always preferred to do so as quietly as possible. Language was to be translated there, it was said, the very worst that a language can be exposed to and a certain violence was unavoidable. The hardest of all for language: to lose its meaning, this meaning that the words so eagerly want to hang on to. Any meaning! There was nothing for it, the words must push past, one by one and quite alone, through the narrow pass. In what way would the language go under, in what shapes would it rise again? Would these remnants once more grasp at each other, catch each other's hands, once more make something that could resemble a meaning?

There's So Much I Miss!

There's so much I miss:
I miss my own wants.
My down-at-heel selfishness,
my obsession with being always
at the center of my own flame.
What do I wish for myself now?
A thin blouse with pointed collar
and a fluttering skirt,
mermaid-hair and mussel-combs
I wish for myself a dancer's feet
and her muscular thighs,
As long as the music plays
she lives breathless and eager
and her heart beats boundlessly
out of time with the music.
What do I wish for myself now?
What's on offer in the shops?
What sort of hunger is there for me?
What sort of hunger,
What sort of thirst?

dly Sins Do You Still Desire Me?

Deadly sins do you still desire me?
Anger do you want to blossom in me?
To send the blood to my cheeks
and make by heart accelerate.
Envy's brief sting,
do you want to strike me,
let me rage in vain
for a different life.
I want to feel pride and walk with pride's padded neck,
I want to feel the sweet sting of bitter love in my body,
and rest a while on the black-market rugs of the flatterers.
I want to feel how stealth makes my brain labor
and how excess seizes me in a voluptuous craving.
Deadly sins do you desire me?
Can you still work in me!

To Journey Like Marlow

What do I care about the mirrored halls, the capital cities,
what do I care about the hissing swans
floating on their mirror of innocence.
To journey like Marlow, like an insect,
towards implacability, the scalps, redemption,
enclosed by primeval forests, trapped in his hull.

Ascendancy in Scorpio

With ascendancy in Scorpio
I feel the desire to dominate
to seize love for myself by force.
My failure and my rage are so great
I must call the deadly sins to my help
and invent new monastic vows: Riches, Fertility and Revolt!

Here in Akra,
desire is always at the center
This desire for memories, any.
To love something and desire it,
to be denied it and disintegrate,
into the letters of the alphabet, into the bones of the skeleton,
to rise again as something else
a silent earth with no meaning,
to walk through the narrow pass,
but memory after memory still intact,
the memory of the deadly sins, their ravenous defiance,
exorbitance, jealousy, gormandizing.

The letters of the alphabet can never help me.
They fall apart like the cards of tired conjurors,
used-up, played-out, frayed-apart,
the letters that would sew me into a new meaning,
and adorn me with this crown, "the only one,"
as if language were the beginning of seclusion,
as if seclusion began in the letters
but I was from the beginning already secluded,
and began to spell myself to a new meaning.

Anguish

Why does anguish scrape me to the bone?
Why does anguish interest itself in me?
I feel an itch in my breast
and a sore under my ribs,
anguish is a gaunt prison,
a foul solitary cell furnished with a pounding heart,
anguish is all that can happen to me,
and all that has already happened.

The red-haired nurse lay installed in the solarium coffin,
she rose with her white skin reddened, corroded.
Your voice on the phone is lustreless and alien.
Now all is gone that was tiger, poppy.

As One Acknowledges Dream and Exile

Night has now come and I acknowledge you
as one acknowledges dream and exile.
Here I spoke in all the tongues that were,
Here I was exorbitant and many,
I poured myself into tall glasses and drank,
and I kicked my shadow before me,
I acknowledge you and you fail to bless me,
you don't know who I am though I describe myself to you
as relentlessly as the drip that hollows out the stone,
I write down a story, a blessing.

Bless me in return! Prepare me a bed!
Let me slap your face, let me be in doubt,
let me swear new vows that cancel the old ones,
Vows of Wealth, the duress of kindness,
Let me love you, as it is fitting for me,
as it is fitting for you.
And I split you. From top to toe.

Not even you can shut the door to my house.
My house stands open to the brawl of the street.
It all flies in through the door, wind and rubbish,
faithful prophets, and doubters and drunkards,
the stink of stale drink fills the hallway,
hair and nose-blood and reiterations,
evening chill, and white flowers stolen from churchyards,
Steal no more now, the names of people should stick to them
and not clothe your new novels, your novels of duress.

Kjell Espmark

In the Hospital It's Two O'clock

Enter the room, double.
Hover at the bedside, double.
"Someone to see you, Mr. Ancker!"
A groan among the blanket's flakes.
Motionless on the bed, eyes closed, the invalid
rises towards the visitor
gropes over cheeks and clothes
tries to assemble it all
into something he recognizes.
The nurse strokes the blanket: "Mr. Ancker!"
Laboriously he faces outwards
extricates a grin from the sheet:
"Well, if it isn't you!"
His head is shaved, rubber tubes and horns of glass.
"It's long since."
The echo carries through neglected years.
"What lovely strawberries you've brought!"
Fingering the grapes.
The room throbs to his headache.
"I'm seeing double, you know."

Motionless on the bed he's standing at the window
staring down at his divided Stockholm:
in winter light two fragile cities
which have glided a handsbreadth apart.
Spires emerging from spires
crowds hurrying out of themselves.

"What lovely strawberries."
The visitor's heart rattles, double and dry.
The language the invalid's fumbling in
echoes with childhood summers.
"That was nice of you."
It's not much he wants:
a window that doesn't glide out of the window
a hand that remains in itself.

Content with five centimeters' coherence
at eye-level.
It's denied him.

When the Earth Was Still Open

A blackened corner of the cemetery
already bears its cross: Matthias Ancker, lost.
Each one alone in driving snow.
Divided, a handsbreadth behind themselves
the mourners stand round this black box
that refuses to sink in the earth
hangs in the air
while the clods tumble in the pit.
He actually leans over the edge
grabs the priest's collar and refuses!
They try persuasion, a frozen mumbling.
He pretends to agree to the ceremony.
But then when everything's said or unsaid
and they shake hands and part
he keeps them company
this way and that
not really much thinner
than those who are trying to mourn him.

Kjell Espmark

Monday Morning at the Teacher's Desk

Only the one hand up.
The white leaves wait in the haze.
The neon tubes sizzle and clack
over the faces as thin
as the whispers at the back of class.
And the stink of damp wool!

"According to Reuter strong forces
have reached Thermopylae, the lock of Greece."
Carefully they stalk about in the poem.
Some turn over the words like stones
and leer at Karin Boye in the heather
where she cowers under the weight of the century.
But the searchers are out in vain
haven't a hope of catching her.
Well, what about Thermopylae?
Only the one hand in the air.

The King of the Persians, scourge of the earth
screams in the microphones;
the voice rises and breaks.
They bring up the year '41.
The teacher knows, among *his* memories:
tanks clattering into antiquity
parachutes drifting over Crete like dandelion seeds—
hi, we save Greek stamps!

But what does history say to you and to you?

The glint from a Persian shield
shines into Gunilla's morning world
with its brown tones and distant footfalls
and father up from the table in a rage.
His hand clenches and opens round his serviette.

What one says can be grasped only
by someone who has use for it.
What a terrible resistance.

And what are *you* up to?
The rascal answers with a sly laugh
he's on the other side, unseen,
a Xerxes with a cooling penknife in his pocket.

The teacher's flow of words divides
in twenty tongues. And his Monday loathing
blizzards through twenty worlds.
In some of them it feels fresh. He sees
a class of bone fragments and damp wool.
He himself has twenty faces
all of them incomplete.

They Seek Shelter

The commissioner and his suite
have been nailed to the threshold:
What an infernal row in here.

Ragged cries
rough gestures
out of nothing.

What kind of agency is this?

Loose nails gleam scratch
for chinks openings
that would give an advantage.

Gnawing like rats
Groping like earwigs
Grating and muttering.

The commissioner defends himself
smeared with almost invisible fingers
hairless, with bad eczema.
He's condemned to stay on this landing
with promises as the only language possible.

Do people really live here?

In order to clarify the situation
they pour plaster into the holes in the air.
As when they dug out Pompeii.
The whiteness hardens into human movements
something like outstretched hands
some running, perhaps with open mouths
and heads thrown back
but clearly not running fast enough.

The most distinct of the plaster fragments
is that woman sitting writing
as if filling in on a form
her name and address in pre-existence
in big angular letters.
Her thumb is bent back pressing the pen.
Seems to be a child sitting by her.
It has her heart on its lap
sticks its finger in and laughs.
O yes, that fragment of cheek and mouth
distinctly has the shape of laughter.
The mother has no face.
But with her shoulders asks:
Who are you
that you promise us a place in reality
some day in a remote chronology?

The Emigrants

Do we darken the night sky for you
with our jerking procession of caravans, rusted
cars, creaking bicycles, dogs and bundles?
Do we become motes in the big telescope
with our tattered rags, grimy infants at the breast—
the unborn, behind, can't catch up.
No, you can see the stars straight through us
through this clamorous multitude
thin as a promise
and driven away since the morning of time.
Nowhere are we allowed to burden
the cosmic community tax
or lower the value of the neighboring villas.
Try in the next galaxy, you said.
We are trying. We reconnoiter for you.
Our timeless life
is an experiment in homelessness.
We made our way through your language.
Our hands were shaped into picklocks
by all your locked doors.
Our faces became feigned innocence
before all that suspicion.
We made our way through.
And if you hear signals on car-horns and frying pans
from years beyond time and reason
we'll have found a new continent for you.

With my hat over my face
I rest in the grass. It's always with us
even among the furthest stars.
Willow-herb up through my breast. Quaking-grass.
The front of the procession
has the same color as the darkness.
I myself am among the last.
Hear them, the steps on the gravel, squeaking wheels
the wailing of infants, all those noises
we've had with us, almost worn out now.
We're trying in the next galaxy.

All Roads Seem to Lead Here

You who stare at us out of the emptiness
without our being able to see you—
come and help us!
Perhaps you are the missing part.
Like that one crawling here on his knees
and he no more than knees.
They're all coming with what they have
from all ages.
I, who climbed to this ledge,
am nails mostly, split and bent
by eternal speeches in defense.
I must have belonged to the drunken killers.
But now I am here and needed.

Look at the limb shuffling this way
almost stiff with the pleasure of massacre.
Has broken free from him who tore it off.
Almost usable.
Scrape the blood from the cobblestones
and bring it into this moment.
Don't spill any.
Pull the guts from the mongrel's jaw
carefully lay them in order in the cart
and pull it into this minute
by chance open, like a forgotten back gate.
The dismembered man shall be restored.

But the bits aren't enough!
Stockholm is a throng of emptiness
blasted houses chafing against blasted houses
on an area smaller than a scream.
Nowhere is it denser than here.
Yet the bits aren't enough.

Search in what is not,
among meager traces which are not,
of close combat and madness
of limbs tossed to all quarters
a concentric despair.
Search. Search behind if and not.
Each step takes a thousand years!
Search in the wind which is not wind.
As if. As if again.
As if.

It Must Be Tiresias' House

I guess you want to meet the old fellow
to have a peep into the future.
It's the old errand for anyone
making his way down to us shadows.
But you must content yourself with the boards here.
We have nailed him in.
It's nothing to make a story of.
He just began talking one day
of a whiteness so intense it could be heard.
He said he could see the absurd.
What exists out there doesn't exist, he said.
It is present in the sense
that it *cannot* exist.
That thought finds no hold in one's head.
He said that he waited for ages
for the rustle of leaves.
But there were no trees there.
And the agitated murmur of men
was neither murmur nor men.
There was only a whitened moment
that went on and on
while his body was more and more tense.
Like some kind of patience with one.
We just couldn't listen to more.
So we boarded up his raised hands
the holes that were his eyes
and the mouth that grew old as he spoke.
We consider much is achieved
if we keep him silent.

Kjell Espmark

He's Sitting on a Bench in the Past

I took you for another
when you came in the burning stairway.
Your shadow looked like an axeman's.
I am familiar with the axe, you see.
Had it day after day in my throat
a prolonged beheading. Month after month.
The executioner aimed badly, thought
I could be parted from the song all the same.
I refused.
He gave me a place here while I lived.

The axe was lifted sky-high.
His neck sinews tautened like string.
His sweaty chest was trembling.
I saw Stockholm thicken round me
where I lay on the rough paving stones.
The harried crowds of Iron Square
made way for cholera-churls and soldiers,
journeymen, shop-maids, carpenters.
A city which carried its lost within itself
stood bowed over me and gave me its strength.
The axe fell.
I refused.
Never was the song more my own.

One night in March he gave up.
Now I can move freely.
As you hear from the others
my dialect is already current here.
Are the vaults too low for song, you mean?
That's what makes song possible.
If you renounce your listening
you'll hear the fierce music.

An Artist's Journey to the Grave

He defends himself despairingly in the open grave.
Shovel after shovelful of silence
falls over his face
creeps into his nose and senses
seeps through his open head
and rattling down slows his heartbeat.
He's talking, trying to persuade.
As if it were his life
to enable others to see
when they only think they see.
He tries to sit up
open his mouth to a scream:
I won't! I'm still alive!
I've much still to do.
A shovel's emptied in his mouth
and scatters what was almost words.
Those standing in the place of the mourners
have stiff cancelled faces
with lilac stains in the gold. And smell bad.
They've gone rigid in mid-movement.
Since they can't hear him
there's no cry in his mouth.
Space with its heavy gilt coating
is quite deaf. The shapes round him
get ready to go. Set in order
their gold-leaf features and thoughts.
But their bliss is transparent;
a text is about
to emerge from the stained skin.
Their kingdom, these circles have another name!
In the silence that tumbles over him
over his parrying arms
he feels, with his mouth full of muddy silence,
insight approaching. But their deafness stops him.
For lack of response
he can't grasp what he almost senses.

Beside Her Desk is the Desk

She's listening with her whole body.
The teacher's lips are moving. And she hears
yet misses his words by a few inches
like trying to catch hold of a stone in water.
There's another world, a handsbreadth from hers.
Right against the map of Sweden
there hangs a map of *Sweden*—
the same towns and jagged lakes
the same yellow and green fields
yet a country shimmering and inaccessible.
They're discussing something now, their mouths in motion.
Of course she can hear. But what's really said
flies sparkling past her ears
to those living in the right country.

Yet she can catch them in the interval
with her sniffling story of daddy being picked up
struggling, pulled out every way.
And mother tried to hide herself in her hands.
Everything's sold for twenty wrinkled laughs.
Talks, straddling, stockings rumpling.

But nothing's changed by her success.
When she tries to take her place in *their* talk
she stumbles into that thin membrane
separating the world from *the world*
and that smile which hurts so much
because it's not intended to be seen.
If she could wangle herself into their Sweden
and carefully sit down among them
would her chair not change into a *chair*
and herself become quite real?
One step to the side is all she needs.
But finds not even a word for that step.
And the classroom knows: she'll never find it.
The language between these four walls
knows her life to come.

She can struggle till she's pulled out every way.
In this amiably inexorable grammar
each has his final place.

The Director of the Environment's Secret Journey

One day in September—air pressure 1005 millibar—
he makes his way down into the future
just as King Alexander in the story
was lowered into the sea in a barrel of glass
(gloomily gazing out at the huge whale
and men at pasture in the deep's floating forests).
He must at last find out for himself
and put an end to the nuclear squabble.
While the greasy lines run out
he sees through the bottle-green glass
the two deformed asssistants at the windlass
exchange a glance that makes him swallow hard
then shrink to nothing.
He has down with him some borrowed experts
who thoughtfully formulate the opinions
their place in the dialogue prescribes.
Still nothing unsettling in the world outside the glass.
The phosphorescing cities are growing
largely according to plan.
A kind of terrace, it seems.
At least the vessel stops sinking.
But what in God's name is this!
Flat against the glass they stare into the absurd.
Faces like sparklers
now here now there.
A woman, close-to, wants to say something.
But her voice is an incomprehensible crackle.
With awkward gestures instead of hands
she seems to warn of something that can't be seen.
She has her children around her. As if they branched out
like a mycelium, uncheckable.
The travellers are afflicted by such trembling
their understanding comes loose in its sockets.
They gasp for words.
One of them hits on a phrase—"in a wider context.."
And that saves them. As soon as they have a tongue in their head
they can defend themselves against what they see.

Their language is a huge filter.
Now the sparkling souls outside the glass
can be allowed to witness. They're at once simplified
to abstractions, can be recognized
as the least important values in the calculation.
A signal's given. And the vessel rises.
Their thoughts move more nimbly.
Soon they can see their boat and its green
bubbly twisted faces
which already feel they know
the pacifying report.

They Don't Even Take Shelter

What an endless procession towards the city.
Clowns, tinkers, swindlers, ragmen,
car dealers without cars, drunkards.
The glowing walls, the inexorable towers
in the distance are growing in the thoughts of all.
The heavenly sewage-smell already reaches them
at twenty kilometers. Sweeter than honey.
What do they hope for?
Work, a bundle of straw on the floor,
half a square meter for their life?
Meaningless.
For each step they take nearer the city
they must relinquish a piece of themselves.
They belong to under-history
where not even the *word* revolt exists.
The crowd is tight and thin like a Dürer engraving.
Around them crows circle
over colorless acres, waiting.
From wheels nailed up
on the posts along the road
they hear the parching cries of those
who tried to enter glory
on their own terms.
But the migrants don't look up.
Their muddy gaze hides
in the mud of the road.
Think with your feet!
One hardly dares even to glance at the distant walls
that must be trembling in the mist.
Each one of those pulsating bundles
counts itself worth at least
the coin we're born with in our fist.
But demands also a place in reality.
In their multitude they seem unconquerable.
Are always facing a headwind
are made for leaning forward.
The only color they know is brown.

Those at the front, approaching the merciless gates
are already walking into their invisibility.

Family Gathering

This park
with its over-bright floating tree-tops
and its drifting cow-parsley
round the semblance of an inn
is a chance meeting-place.
One comes here with a bit of oneself,
a fragment of anonymous suit,
a pinch of watchful courtesy
and warped memories of the family—
to test them against others' misunderstanding
in the hope that the bits can be pieced into
a pattern beyond one's own experience:
a family portrait
disclosing the individual's place.
And showing a stump of freedom's boundary.

Now, they assemble here for a photograph,
an already over-exposed company.
The whitened children in different directions
at once. The dead, enticed out
by the rank scent of the questions,
are looking for their places
in those at present living. Also uninvited
kin jostle, interbred, irrelevant
to the day's festivities but hard to turn away.
In the back row stands the narrator.
A farmer from the time of Charles the Fifteenth
tries to come into him, deceptively like
the Indian chief Geronimo, with deep-set
merciless eyes and a face of leather
in the sparse preacher's beard.
Is visible when looked at. Of course—
he tries to press his eye-balls
into the younger's, to see through them
or give them his sight. The younger parries,
grasps the aged beard.

Wait. Here's a yellowed photo
that sheds light on the situation:
grandfather and the boy at the grindstone.
The old man turns the handle,
his dwindling powers seek a way
through spindle and stone to the young heart.
The boy resists, less and less gets through
the thinning edge pressed against the stone
Within the old man: an emptiness
crying for his favorite daughter Märit.
Was at her death he 'went Evangelical'
and made himself more and more like the prophets
who have nothing to repent. He is well-read
in *The Knowledgeable Schoolmaster*. His experience,
gleaming, half-transparent
like the outhouse window behind them,
he wants to transmit through this alien boy
too fine in his Sunday best. He'll write, that's sure,
let the old man see with cleansed eyes,
speak with young and steady voice.
There's so much knowledge to glean,
I'll show the lad how we read the tracks of God.
There's so much he wants in others.
But the edge pressed to the stone thins.
The emigrating soul is checked
by the steel's ever sharper resistance
and is scattered in sparks between them.

Such a resistance in the grouping, too.
The living brush off the thoughts of the dead,
a haze of flies that persists, persists.
Ready to click. Should be possible
to see the real family gathering here—
the gathering of the dead in each and all,
how they jostle and wrangle in each and all,
how they bargain, give and take,
and at last agree on an identity.

To grasp what's happening here
one must identify the dead. A general fervor.
Some push into the circle: Lasse from Espnäs
with two skins in the 1542 accounts.
An unexpected relation is Jens Joensson,
the family renegade. Lost his farm at Öhn
for taking the Swedish oath in the Kalmar war.
And this is still further off-scene:
lichen for a beard and a gleam on his face
from the ash-house where his wife is screaming
alone with the flames: the door locked
by a strut—fallen? put there?
He was acquitted but the prosecutor demands
a retrial—after three centuries—
elbows forward through the crowd, embittered.
By mistake assails the solid farmer
who seized a burning log from the fire
when the wolves nuzzled the door in 1815
and thrust it in the pack-leader's teeth.
What was it he recognized?

Countryfolk from Skåne and a throng of strangers
mix with these hundreds from Jämtland.
This farmer, without the family features,
is the village artist
who painted his dream on wooden beaters and swingles.
The stone lion under his arm is clearly Assyrian
and shows how long his art has been on the way:
the legs are worn quite out.
His mother lingers in the background
among the heavily pruned willows.
Will only, half-averted through shyness,
let it be known that after all she slept with the Count
and that certain noses and talents
should be interpreted accordingly.
She is one of the few to have any color:
ephemeral pastel, too much pink.
—What nonsense! She who protests
must have been born a grandmother.

Straddles as if she were very fat.
What in God's name is she holding the belt for?
Can a descendant's memory of a good hiding
distort the past that much?
Is history so soft?
Just what she thought!
Here the serfdom of the dead is passed over.
They're there, in the daily toil:
it's from them that strength comes.
Even so they have to stand there
where the view of the living insists.
And may be seen only in the twisted guise
a later person lends them.
But now they demand justice!

Justice? This man has something to do with her, it seems,
but what he holds out is a rope:
—This is my justice.
No descendant will see that knot.
My death became...heart failure,
a decent fever. And the bottles
which were a name for my self-contempt,
these they have swept up.
Just as I tidied myself out of the world.

Catching his sick glance
as he tosses the rope over a branch.
One is expected to stare at the swinging loop
while he furtively slips round one
to slip his hands from behind
into one's own. Resistance!

But where should the resistance be applied?
These scattered notices about the dead
fall in with the wishes of the living
and have nothing further to tell
of the mafia's gathering in one. The real context,
the one focused in this burning face,
remains inaccessible. The eye
leaves all these coaxed witnesses.

And so the pattern appears:
voices and steps from the meeting families
crystalize in a shape
which *should* be the narrator
but is the over-bright figure beside him,
so like it must be a twin,
only with another loyalty in his back,
most like a bureaucrat
with professionally open skull,
honest as wool, of course,
listening in to the center of power, though.
But that other one does not exist.
The uncertainty of the system
has produced a half-meter miss
and an unexpected freedom.
The aged figures around
are clearly disturbed
by this limit to participation.

Round the too-white coffee-table
under the trees' wandering tops
a world clamors: centuries and climates
throng in the park. The hand
that stirs in the quite immaterial cup
absently frees itself from a thousand hands.
Shining with their energy.
He who tells this shares the features of many
in the quarrelsome gathering.
And they demand their right in him!
But the movement in what he says
is another word for freedom.

The Departure From Grenada

Such a crush to push through:
a throng of donkey-braying and despair
along the slope. Each question
is met by a face that abdicates. Carts
piled with the recollections of eight centuries
vanish down through the valley. A whole chapter
of the past is carried off. And the present
is already hard to grasp. Seen from here
there's not one splinter of wood in the carts,
not one creak in the wheels.
The senses slowly draw away,
turn back a moment
and draw away. The warm
stone that knows each line
in the pulsating palm
gives all its impressions back
to those drawing away
and becomes intangible.
Here's the abandoned Moor's palace,
barely in touch with the ground.
It has fading walls of air and light,
dissolving floors of light and water.

The loneliness in the Court of the Lions
has its painful center here.
The swallows beat through the head, in and out
among thoughts that won't solidify to foliage.
This is the place for a leave-taking.
And he who stands here is caught unawares
by a stranger's sorrow.

This is absurd: how can the cypresses,
those self-controlled green flames,
leave this red earth?
And become only a word.

They are already only a word.

And the swaying greenery a moment ago,
that temperate philosophy
where the concept acquired a scent
and the logic a tangible structure?
There's still an inkling of the mild teacher—
quick now. We slip out of the lecture.
To the gloom behind the hall of the ambassadors
where all is turned to the observer's eyes
and therefore nothing observed. No here:
the bathroom. Hand brushes against hand
and the flames flit down the secret skin.
Nothing visible, not even
the suddenly heavy breath.
You remember? I do.

But then it's someone else's memory
groping into mine!
This burning expectation
belongs to a lurching cart
that was blue, keep off, it's clearly blue
and the laborious breathing
mists the glass, blurs the world.
A stranger remembers in what I remember.
And for one moment he becomes me.
The same trembling steps together
into the dark room long ago.
Steps long since gone but still here
vehement as the blackbird's song.

A shy voice, it no longer exists,
it exists, at a distance of two meters.
A dress falling to the ground
without ever reaching it
and a shadowy gleaming skin
long since gone, here.
The stranger's memory, within my own.
And this exists, the darkness of these lips
is opened
by virtue of its not existing.

A kingdom visible when lost.

The world does draw away.
Only the forms remain, the leaves flee:
The entire flora of stone round the Court of the Lions—
work of the Christian artist, the Mozarab.
Yes, he was allowed to work here. Remains a moment
under the roof of air shaped like honeycombs
from which the light drips. It slowly rotates,
the octagonal roof. The departed man breathes.
At last his steps follow those of the others
and only the space of the cupola is left,
the emptied sign of tolerance.
A sign already hard to grasp.

The last crowd totters down to the valley,
a vanishing throng of colors and cries
leaving behind a black-and-white silence.
The moist gleam of thought draws away
leaving thought behind.
Now one can see without seeing.
With this abstraction much becomes possible.
Soon one can grasp the whole world
without hearing one single scream.

The wind moves into the emptied lanes.
Over the flayed hills: the wind.
A wind sharp without closeness,
wind that is whining sword-cuts
without even iron over the neck,
wind with a king's grating voice.

I'm Still Called Osip Mandelstam

No, this is not migraine.
It's the remains of an assignment
beating
still in the emptiness.

I just find it so hard to breathe, Nadia.
As if we lay in our bunks
staring at the roof: a throng so dense
it finds no place in the word 'throng.'
This barracks is a mass grave
where we share each other's death. Hear the others'
slow thoughts groping in the room
for a window. Just as clearly
as the smell of urine here.

At last I learned,
dissolved in fever and excrement,
to think with the body.
And the current passing through the room
(where from?) gives me strength.
Someone is breathing for me.

Manage to think I raise myself on one
arm and stare through the window.
Nothing seems to have been changed:
the empty landscape, the lack of oxygen,
the Siberian smell of loneliness—all
the same. Our Land's Father knew to an inch
how death's kingdom is composed. Already lived
as if the land didn't exist.
His eyes just a stiff paranoia to see with,
the moustache just a wolf-grey wrath that scented
another Russia in the middle of his Russia,
a land that makes the land visible.
But the stars low, pliable images
that gave the signals he required.

How those who administer reality
fear poetry: an unexpected resistance
making it possible to see.

They had quite simply to choke my voice.
Snipped me out of readers' memories
the way one cuts a page from the Encyclopedia.
For he whom no-one listens to
is choked by his own words.
Now five deep breaths tell me
you saved my manuscripts
and some read what I wrote. Someone
turns a page: gives me words to see with.
See the empty window-frame. The pail
in the corner: a dented stink of ideology.
I see quite clearly that I'm dead.
I see that changes nothing.
New words make their way from the mouth
and move through the emptiness here.
They'll find me lousy with poetry
although the room was fumigated.

No-one writes after their death, you say.
But that's wrong, Nadia.
If I stopped
your heart would stop beating
and Russia remain a desolate idea.

You don't dare believe?
I see your doubt branching
outside the window, a hinted green.
My word settles swaying down in it,
a few trial notes, an arabesque
forcing the indeterminate green to leaves,
each one precise, with five fingers.
For one minute perhaps the word turns
this non-existent tree
into a maple

and the tree turns the word into a goldfinch
swaying in the branch-tip. No note
is where it could be expected.

The road is for a moment clear—
but it's the road from Vladivostok.
And you are standing on it.
Feel you standing staring in my darkness.
Don't stop breathing for me!
I raise my hand in your breeze.
The muddy plain holds a Mediterranean.
The fins of dolphins deep under the earth
plough without pause, like the writer's hand.
A Crete with heights of gleaming skin
is caught in the clay. The waves rise,
scarcely able to hold back their 'Yes'—

Darkness. It's much too soon.
My lonely thought is cold.
How did the concept 'cloak' come into my hands?
Must be you who sent it.
So worn it is. I've nothing to mend it with.
But it is a cloak all right.
I quickly wrap it round the shivering land.
Must have more patience.
Must begin with what's near.

Now I shall think of a humble word:
earwig. Scampers on the window-sill
no, where one could expect a window-sill,
pedantically precise
but impossible to foresee. Seems
to move unscathed out and in of death,
out of my world, into yours.
Now it short-cuts across a finger.
Which for a moment exists. The word's
resistance is a sudden joy.

The Secret Meal

Swept sky, swept shore: always
the same decreed oblivion. The Baltic
a mere word: empty waves, weightless sand.
A wind without integrity
roams upon the waters
like the Party's spirit.
All that grows here is barbed-wire.

But unceasing this murmur
from earth and space, a surge of voices
giving meaning to the undefined branches
we absent-mindedly stoke into the fire,
the damp shoes I pull off,
and the wine poured into my glass.

As if we still sat in the clamorous
mosaic in Fulvia's villa
when the province was called Africa:
pieces of will, clauses of stone
in a timeless gathering
forbidden each moment.
Fragments of hands out-stretched
to something in the middle that's torn away
but belongs to this sign of resistance.

Quiet! The incautious plover
is several seconds before his cry,
takes a step back, stands motionless
with his neck-feathers blown forward by the wind.
Bringing news to us of our helplessness.

Above us still the emperor's heaven, arch upon arch
of cornflower-blue squares, decision
upon decision making themselves. Fasces
of light from the high windows.

Who am I? A bit of an M,
an anger without an object
and a pair of Chaplin-shoes on the run.
Thought I was lecturing: flying
from house to house. The listeners' faces
grey as stubborn snow. What was I talking about?
My memory is transparent December.
A faded scrap of newspaper
where our very language
is herded on the back of a truck.

Only the murmur makes us comprehensible:
as if someone arrived out of nothing,
took a few dragging steps up the shore
and sat down where you should be,
trembling drops on dark eyelids—
and I saw you, for the first time.

So many breathing among us.
The shaking glass I raise to my mouth
gathers mist upon mist along its edge.

So many hands mingling with ours.
These fingers seem to be children's, they stretch
as if they wanted out of the goods wagon crush.
These are an old woman's, they grope
as if they claimed life from the drifting smoke.
They all reach towards the sign in the middle: the bread
that rests in the air without falling.

Like the moment before one discovers
a new and unstained continent: wing-beats,
spice-scents, cool vertigo. Hold back
those words that start an empire.

They seem to catch the smell of bread
and the rustle of approaching birds. Always
the same inquisitive steps. Two-edged axes,
bayonets. A face is a crime.
And we are close to an identity.
As when barricades of cobblestones
are levelled with the ground, again, again,
until the stones trampled down in the sand
at last show human features.

Listen. In the wind
a wind rises. We have life to claim.
Inside the abstract wave
comes a wave of grey and gold. Rips
with the noise of a letter at the censor's,
flings up in spray, almost water—
and finds its way through. Suddenly, a scent
long-since snatched away is there again,
warm and dry: thyme and bedstraw, words
dividing into stiffening colors. Depths
lent from an elated memory: grove
behind grove, paler and paler grey.
The empty place among us speaks.

And our empty hands reach
towards the middle and break a crumbling
power . Share it out among crane-flies and doubters.
Saliva of many ages moistens the bite.
Can this year too be cancelled?

The pale concept 'day'
is filled with evening light,
a thinned-out slightly crackled ochre
on its way since 1600
to make the world come into being.

In our incompleted mouths
the scattered questions crowd.
We are scarcely here
yet there is speech in us.
The words burn upon our lips.

Tomas Tranströmer

The Forgotten Captain

We have many shadows. I was walking home
in the September night when Y
climbed out of his grave after forty years
and kept me company.

At first he was quite empty, only a name
but his thoughts swam
faster than time ran
and caught up with us.

I put his eyes to my eyes
and saw war's ocean.
The last boat he captained
took shape beneath us.

Ahead and astern the Atlantic convoy crept,
the ships that would survive
and the ships that bore the Mark
(invisible to all)

while sleepless days relieved each other
but never him.
Under his oilskin, his life-jacket.
He never came home.

It was an internal weeping that bled him to death
in a Cardiff hospital.
He could at last lie down
and turn into a horizon.

Goodbye, eleven-knot convoys! Goodbye, 1940!
Here ends world history.
The bombers were left hanging.
The heathery moors blossomed.

A photo from early this century shows a beach.
Six Sunday-best boys.
Sailing-boats in their arms.
What solemn airs!

The boats that became life and death for some of them.
And writing about the dead—
that too is a game, made heavy
with what is to come.

Six Winters

1.

In the black hotel a child is asleep.
And outside: the winter night
where the wide-eyed dice roll.

2.

An elite of the dead became stone
in Katarina Churchyard
where the wind shakes in its armor from Svalbard.

3.

One wartime winter when I lay sick
a huge icicle grew outside the window.
Neighbor and harpoon, unexplained memory.

4.

Ice hangs down from the roof-edge.
Icicles: the upside-down Gothic.
Abstract cattle, udders of glass.

5.

On a side-track an empty railway carriage.
Still. Heraldic.
With the journeys in its claws.

6.

Tonight snow-haze, moonlight. The moonlight-jellyfish itself
is floating before us. Our smiles
on the way home. Bewitched avenue.

The Nightingale in Badelunda

In the green midnight at the nightingale's northern limit. Heavy leaves hang in trance, the deaf cars race towards the neon-line. The nightingale's voice rises without wavering to the side, it is as penetrating as a cock-crow, but beautiful and free of vanity. I was in prison and it visited me. I was sick and it visited me. I didn't notice it then, but I do now. Time streams down from the sun and the moon and into all the tick-tock-thankful clocks. But right here there is no time. Only the nightingale's voice, the raw resonant notes that whet the night sky's gleaming scythe.

Early May Stanzas

A May wood. The invisible removal load,
    my whole life, like a haunting here. Birds in song.
        In the silent pools, midge-larvae—
            their dancing furious question-marks.

The same places I escape to, and the same words.
    Cool sea breeze. And the ice-dragon licks the back
        of my neck while sunlight blazes.
            The load is burning with chilly flames.

use

I am a mummy at rest in the blue coffin of the forests, in the
perpetual roar of engines and rubber and asphalt.

What happened during the day sinks, the lessons are heavier
than life.

The wheelbarrow rolled forward on its single wheel and I myself tra-
velled on my spinning psyche, but now my thoughts have
stopped going round and the wheelbarrow has got wings.

At long last, when space is black, a plane will come. The passengers
will see the cities beneath them glittering like the gold of
the Goths.

Streets in Shanghai

1.

The white butterfly in the park is read by many.
I love that cabbage-white as if it were a fluttering corner of truth itself!

At dawn the crowds get our silent planet going with their running.
The park fills with people. To each one there are eight faces polished like jade, for every situation, for the avoidance of mistakes.

To each one, also, the invisible face that mirrors "something one doesn't talk about."
Something that turns up in tired moments and is acrid like a mouthful of adder-brandy with its lingering scaly aftertaste.

The carp in the pond move perpetually, they swim while they sleep, they are models for the faithful: always in motion.

2.

It's midday. The washing flutters in the grey sea-wind high above the cyclists
who come in dense shoals. Notice the labyrinths to left and right!

I'm encircled by written signs I can't interpret, I'm totally illiterate.
But I've paid what I should and have receipts for everything.
I've accumulated about me so many illegible receipts.
I'm an old tree with withered leaves that hang on and can't fall to the earth.

And a puff of air from the sea makes all those receipts rustle.

3.

At dawn the crowds get our silent planet going with their tramping.
We are all aboard the street. It is packed like the deck of a ferry.
Where are we going? Are there enough tea-cups? We can count ourselves
lucky
    getting aboard this street!
It's a thousand years before the birth of claustrophobia.

Behind each one walking here there glides a cross which wants to catch
    up on us, overtake us, unite with us.
Something which wants to creep up behind us and cover our eyes and
    whisper "Guess who!"

We look almost happy out in the sun, while we are bleeding fatally from
    wounds we don't know about.

Deep in Europe

I a dark hull floating between two lock-gates
rest in the hotel bed while the city around me wakens.
The silent clamor and the grey light stream in
and raise me slowly to the next level: the morning.

Overheard horizon. They want to say something, the dead.
They smoke but don't eat, they don't breathe but they keep their voice.
I'll be hurrying through the streets as one of them.
The blackened cathedral, heavy as a moon, causes ebb and flow.

Tomas Tranströmer

Leaflet

The silent rage scribbles on the wall inwards.
Fruit-trees in blossom, the cuckoo calls.
It's spring's narcosis. But the silent rage
paints its slogans backwards in the garages.

We see all and nothing, but straight as periscopes
wielded by the underground's shy crew.
It's the war of the minutes. The blazing sun
stands above the hospital, suffering's parking-place.

We living nails hammered down in society!
One day we shall loosen from everything.
We shall feel death's air under our wings
and become milder and wilder than here.

The Indoors is Endless

It's spring in 1827, Beethoven
hoists his death-mask and sails off.

The grindstones are turning in Europe's
    windmills.
The wild geese are flying northwards.

The north is here, here is Stockholm
floating palaces and hovels.

The logs in the royal fireplace
collapse from Attention to At Ease.

Peace prevails, vaccine and potatoes,
but the city wells breathe heavily.

Privy barrels in sedan chairs like paschas
are carried by night over the North Bridge.

The cobblestones make them stagger
mamselles loafers gentlemen.

Implacably still, the sign-board
with the smoking blackamoor.

So many islands, so many rowing
with invisible oars against the current!

The channels open up, April May
and sweet honey dribbling June.

The heat reaches islands far out.
The village doors are open, except one.

The snake-clock's pointer licks the silence.
The rock slopes glow with geology's
    patience.

[handwritten margin note:] The music of Beethoven erupts up. The foundry!

It happened like this, or almost.
It is an obscure family tale

about Erik, done down by a curse
disabled by a bullet through the soul.

He went to town, met an enemy
and sailed home sick and grey.

Keeps to his bed all that summer.
The tools on the wall are in mourning.

He lies awake, hears the wooly flutter
of night moths, his moonlight comrades.

His strength ebbs out, he pushes in vain
against the iron-bound tomorrow.

And the God of the depths cries out of
        the depths
"Deliver me! Deliver yourself!"

All the surface action turns inwards.
He's taken apart, put together.

The wind rises and the wild rose-bushes
catch on the fleeing light.

The future opens, he looks into
the self-rotating kaleidoscope

sees indistinct fluttering faces
family faces not yet born.

By mistake his gaze strikes me
as I walk around here in Washington

among grandiose houses where only
every second column bears weight.

White buildings in crematorium style
where the dream of the poor turns to ash.

The gentle downward slope gets steeper
and imperceptibly becomes an abyss.

robots building
robots in my
dream

dream
machines

A god torn apart
every day
put together
in dreams
every night

torn out of
Hollywood
nights

Mill wheels of
Beethoven

For Turn through
The gas-chamber's
nightmare
with smokestacks
and taffeta dresses

I stammer
in ferns of roses
my psyche goes
round like a
wheel

Vermeer

No protected world...Just behind the wall the noise begins,
the inn is there
with laughter and bickering, rows of teeth, tears, the din of bells
and the deranged brother-in-law, the death-bringer we all must
    tremble for.

The big explosion and the tramp of rescue arriving late
the boats preening themselves on the straits, the money creeping down
    in the wrong man's pocket
demands stacked on demands
gaping red flowerheads sweating premonitions of war.

In from there and right through the wall into the clear studio
into the second that's allowed to live for centuries.
Pictures that call themselves 'The Music Lesson'
or 'Woman in Blue Reading a Letter'—
she's in her eighth month, two hearts kicking inside her.
On the wall behind is a crumpled map of Terra Incognita.

Breathe clamly...An unknown blue material nailed to the chairs.
The gold studs flew in with incredible speed
and stopped abruptly
as if they had never been other than stillness.

Ears sing, from depth or height.
It's the pressure from the other side of the wall.
It makes each fact float
and steadies the brush.

It hurts to go through walls, it makes you ill
but it is necessary.
The world is one. But walls...
And the wall is part of yourself—
we know or we don't know but it's true for us all
except for small children. No walls for them.

The clear sky has leant itself against the wall.
It's like a prayer to the emptiness.
And the emptiness turns its face to us
and whispers
'I am not empty, I am open.'

Romanesque Arches

Inside the huge romanesque church the tourists jostled in
the half darkness.
Vault gaped behind vault, no complete view.
A few candle-flames flickered.
An angel with no face embraced me
and whispered through my whole body:
"Don't be ashamed of being human, be proud!
Inside you vault opens behind vault endlessly.
You will never be complete, that's how it's meant to be."
Blind with tears
I was pushed out on the sun-seething piazza
together with Mr. and Mrs. Jones, Mr. Tanaka and Signora
Sabatini
and inside them all vault opened behind vault endlessly.

Epigram

The buildings of capital, the hives of the killer bees,
                    honey for the few.
He served there. But in a dark tunnel he unfolded his wings
and flew when no-one was looking. He had to live his life again.

Female Portrait, 19th Century

Her voice is stifled in the clothing. Her eyes
follow the gladiator. Then she herself is
on the arena. Is she free? A gilt frame
                    strangles the picture.

Medieval Motif

Beneath our spell-binding play of faces there waits
inevitably the skull, the poker-face. While
the sun's unhurriedly rolling past in the sky.
                    And the chess continues.

A barber-scissor-like clipping sound from the copse.
The sun's unhurriedly rolling past in the sky.
The game of chess comes to a standstill, in a draw.
                In the rainbow's silence.

Air Mail

On the hunt for a letter-box
I took the letter through the city.
In the big forest of stone and concrete
the straying butterfly flickered.

The flying-carpet of the stamp
the staggering lines of the address
plus my own sealed truth
soaring now over the ocean.

The Atlantic's creeping silver.
The cloud-banks. The fishing-boat
like a spat-out olive-stone.
And the pale scars of the wakes.

Down here work goes slowly.
I ogle the clock often.
The tree-shadows are black ciphers
in the greedy silence.

The truth's there, on the ground
but no-one wants to take it.
The truth's there, on the street.
No-one makes it his own.

Madrigal

I inherited a dark wood where I seldom go. But a day will come when the dead and the living change places. Then the wood will start moving. We are not without hope. The most serious crimes will remain unsolved in spite of the efforts of many policemen. In the same way there is somewhere in our lives a great unsolved love. I inherited a dark wood, but today I'm walking in the other wood, the light one. All the living creatures that sing, wriggle, wag and crawl! It's spring and the air is very strong. I have graduated from the university of oblivion and am as empty-handed as the shirt on the washing-line.

Golden Wasp

The blindworm that legless lizard flows along the porch step
calm and majestic as an anaconda, only the size is different.
The sky is covered with clouds but the sun pushes through.
That kind of day.

This morning she who is dear to me drove away the evil spirits.
As when you open the door of a dark shed somewhere in the south
and the light pours in
and the cockroaches dart off into the corners and up the walls
and are gone—you saw them and you didn't see them—
so her nakedness made the demons run.

As if they never existed.
But they'll come back.
With a thousand hands crossing the lines in the old-fashioned telephone
        exchange of the nerves.

It's the fifth of July. The lupins are stretching up as if
        they wanted to catch sight of the sea.
We're in the church of keeping-silence, in the piety according to no letter.
As if they didn't exist, the implacable faces of the patriarchs
and the misspelling of God's name in stone.

I saw a true-to-the-letter TV preacher who'd piled in the money.
But he was weak now and needed the support of a bodyguard,
who was a well-tailored young man with a smile tight as a muzzle.
A smile stifling a scream.
The scream of a child left alone in a hospital bed when the parents leave.

The divine brushes against a human being and lights a flame
but then draws back.
Why?
The flame attracts the shadows, they fly rustling in and join the flame,
which rises and blackens. And the smoke spreads out black and strangling.
At last only the black smoke, at last only the pious executioner.

The pious executioner leans forward
over the market-place and the crowd that make a grainy mirror
where he can see himself.

The greatest fanatic is the greatest doubter. Without knowing it.
He is a pact between two
where the one is a hundred per cent visible
and the other invisible.
How I hate that expression "a hundred per cent."

Those who can never exist anywhere except on their facades
those who are never absent-minded
those who never open the wrong door and catch a glimpse of the
    Unidentified One.
Walk past them!

It's the fifth of July. The sky is covered with clouds but the sun pushes
    through.
The blindworm flows along the porch step, calm and majestic
            as an anaconda.
The blindworm as if there were no bureaucracy.
The golden wasp as if there were no idolatry.
The lupins as if there were no "hundred per cent."

I know the depth where one is both prisoner and ruler, like Persephone.
I often lay in the stiff grass down there
and saw the earth arch over me.
The vault of the earth.

Often—that's half my life.

But today my gaze has left me.
My blindness has gone away.
The dark bat has left my face and is scissoring around in summer's
            bright space.

Biographical Notes

Lennart Sjögren

Lennart Sjögren (b. 1930) lives on Öland, where he was born and grew up in an agricultural community. In the 1950s he studied art, mainly in Gothenburg, and although he still paints, his main means of expression is poetry. He has now produced nearly twenty books, chiefly of poems but also of short stories, of lyrical prose and of essays.

The poems chosen by Sjögren for a *Selected Poems* in 1980 are longish sequences; formally they are rather loose-limbed and in a note to one of them he explains why so many of this earlier poems were long: "I wrote in an exalted mood, the individual details were so numerous, I wanted to see each one of them clearly before my eyes, together they created a throng." Two of the briefest poems in the book, "The Organ"—

> On a rubbish-heap, on top of stacked cars,
> an organ. Now and then at night it plays.
> A doll puts up its head.
> With raised paws the rats too
> who have their lives here
> in this solemn silence
> listen.

and "The Grass"—

> It's not the scythe which bites the grass
> it's the grass which at last
> eats away the scythe to a blade without steel
> —drugged to rust
> it sleeps then
> in the overgrown grass.

—were accompanied by the following comment:

> Like a panorama painting, the long poem can convey a paradoxical sense of life standing still—as if it were necessary to include all those happenings only to show how closed the world is. The classical, small-scale still-life (a fish, a fruit) corresponds to the short poem—in spite of the limited choice of motif and the narrow range it can feel as if the whole world is suddenly contained there, the view inwards clarified in a quite unsuspected manner.

He adds that the free-standing short poems had emerged only now and then, though in the longer sequences the occasional stanza can function as a short poem on its own, and he cites "The Birch-Leaf" from "The Sea" as an example:

> And the birch-leaf found
> far out to sea
> where it rested
> in its own greening boat.

These remarks struck me as interesting in relation to those aspects of Sjögren's writing which have attracted me as a translator, for in his later collections we can see two distinct genres—in this book I have included examples of both, rather than of the longer earlier works.

On the one hand we have a higher incidence of short poems of the kind which manage to suggest more by saying less, which create a sense of mystery partly because they select the minimum amount of detail instead of aiming to include as much as possible. On the other hand, the more circumstantial leanings of Sjögren's imagination tend to find expression in his short prose pieces (a genre practiced by many Swedish poets): these are highly selective too, of course, perhaps giving us only a part of a possible narrative or a fragment of a situation, but the rhythms here are those of a prose which can accommodate detail and description without strain.

The natural world explored by Sjögren's poems and prose pieces is more shocking and surprising than the world we find in the work of more straightforward nature-poets, and it is also a good deal more uneasy and threatening and destructive than the world often celebrated by poets intent on defending the ecological environment against human marauders. It can be indifferent, not through mere passivity but through absorption in its own decidedly non-pastoral processes. The experience of it which Sjögren gives us has a kaleidoscopic quality, as if we are in touch with a nature which is not quiet wholly biological and not quite wholly spiritual either. Or perhaps we should say both biological and spiritual: in an earlier poem (collected in 1971), addressed to the medieval German sculptor Bernt Notke, Sjögren wrote about dreaming of an alliance between the pious and the fleshly, between the mysterious and the practical, and something of this dream can be sensed behind his work as a whole.

Eva Ström

Eva Ström (b. 1949) studied medicine, specializing in infectious diseases, and worked as a doctor in Kristianstad from 1974 to 1988. She now writes full-time. She has published three collections of poems, one novel, and a book of what she calls "lyrical prose." Recently she has been active as a dramatist, productions including a stage-play and several radio-plays.

Some of her poems spring from her medical experience—or rather, I would say, from experience as a doctor alongside other kinds of experience, such as motherhood. Others grow out of play with nursery-rhyme and fairytale rhythms, images and characters. Many of them are role-poems, spoken by a semi-dramatic persona: her interest in radio-drama can be seen as a natural extension of the earlier poetry. But what gives her work its unity is the power of her imagination, and since the publication of her first volume in 1977 her voice has been one of the most distinctive in Swedish writing. A reviewer of her 1979 collection for instance referred to her as "one of the sharpest and most individual" of the younger poets. And a reviewer of the 1983 volume laid stress on her ability to probe "fundamental questions" and on her "unexpected, surprising and at times inaccessible images."

The style of the first two collections—*The Burning Zeppelin* (1977), whose title refers to the Hindenburg disaster on May 6th, 1937, and *Steinkind* (1979), whose German title literally means "stone-child"—is modified by the time we reach *Akra* (1983). Here the language is less playful, the metaphors fewer, the vocabulary sometimes more down-to-earth, and there are no fairytale or saga personae. This is in keeping with the more austere nature of the spiritual progress explored in the book, a progress into and out of a state of deprivation most readily hinted at in the author's own comments on the title:

"I saw the road to Akra as a desert landscape with a mountain pass and beyond the pass lay Akra. I read Paul Celan's secretive words: *Ein Kranz ward gewunden aus schwärzlichem Laub in der Gegend von Akra.* I read Gunnar Ekelöf, whose Prince Emgion is an *akrit*, a frontier prince, and found there that *akra* really means mountainland, frontierland. My book of poems is about that frontierland, about the way there, about living there, about getting away from it. The journey to Akra has the same implacable character as Marlowe's journey in *The Heart of Darkness*. To live unblessed, unreconciled, in God's absence, is to live in Akra." (*Svenska Dagbladet*, July 17th, 1983). In the course of the same article

Eva Ström wrote: "I've never followed the advice usually given to young authors—on the contrary I've jumped again and again right into the big themes and told the old stories over again."

Kjell Espmark

Kjell Espmark (b. 1930) has taught at Stockholm University since 1964 and has been a member of The Swedish Academy since 1981. In addition to nine collections of poetry, he has published one novel and seven books of literary criticism, including studies of his fellow-poets Artur Lundkvist, Harry Martinson and Tomas Tranströmer and an historical discussion of the decision-making processes behind the Nobel Prize for Literature.

The vision emerging from his poetry, focused on Sweden but with implications of much wider import on a truly European scale, is recreated with a depth of literary, historical and political reference that marks it off from much else in modern Swedish poetry. (We have to look to writers like Gunnar Ekelöf or Östen Sjöstrand to find a similar inclusiveness.) Yet Espmark is anxious we should not regard this as "learned" poetry: the learning is there, yes, but as a resource from which he can draw, not as an end in itself. As Tommy Olofsson stresses in his introduction to Espmark's *Collected Poems* (1987), both the knowledge and the literary skill which Espmark brings to his writing is subordinated to a moral engagement, a deep indignation and an acute capacity for empathy.

Another important aspect of Espmark's poetry is the way in which individual poems, themselves sometimes fairly long, are built into large-scale patterns that gain in significance from book to book. After his first three collections, his main poetic output has gone into two "trilogies." The first set of three contains *Voices in Public* (1968), *Voices under Ground* (1972) and *The Inexorable Paradise* (1975), and all three were republished as one book in 1976. In his Afterword to this book Espmark says he doesn't want readers to become too absorbed in puzzling out the details within the overall structure—though of course those features are not there by accident. Each book contains twenty-five poems with thematic and verbal links creating a symmetrical arrangement where numbers 1 and 25 correspond, as do 2 and 24, 3 and 23, and so on, with number 13 in each book holding a solitary but important position. These correspondences, moreover, run though all three books, so that there are close connections between, say, I:6, I:20, II:6, II:20, III:6 and III:20. In the case of a selection, of course, much of this cross-patterning is unfortunately lost, but the point should nonetheless be made.

The second trilogy contains a smaller number of poems but they are longer: each book has twelve poems. What Espmark gives us is a collection or gallery of what could be described as first-person posthumous portraits, each one being an "attempt" at some kind of life, first on a personal level (*Attempts at Life*, 1979), then on a European scale (*Signs of Europe*, 1982) and finally on a world scale (*The Secret Meal*, 1984).

Tomas Tranströmer

Tomas Tranströmer (b. 1931) grew up in Stockholm and since 1967 he has lived in Västerås, where he works as a psychologist. Ever since the publication of his first collection of poems in 1954 he has had a special position in contemporary Swedish literature, and now he is the Swedish poet who is best known abroad. His reading tours have taken him all over the world and he has been much translated: in addition to shorter selections in over twenty languages, larger selections have appeared in Spanish, Dutch, Hungarian, German and of course in English. Every poem in every collection has been translated into English, and the majority of his poems exist in two or more English versions. He has won many prizes too, the latest including the 1981 Petrach Prize (in West Germany), the 1983 Bonnier Poetry Prize and the 1988 Pilot Prize. and the 1990 *Nordiska rådets pris*.

One thing which makes Tranströmer's poetry so widely accessible (in spite of the loss in translation of its original Swedish music) must be the startling clarity of its imagery and its surprising changes of perspective. He himself has described his poems as meeting-places where sudden connections are made between aspects of reality which conventional uses of language and habitual outlooks tend to keep apart. And Robert Bly has said that Tranströmer's poems "are mysterious because of the distance the images have come to get there."

Something of this quality is present in Tranströmer's entire oeuvre but of course there have been developments, and two of the most significant can perhaps be briefly described as follows. First, we can see some attempt to be gradually more specific about the central space or crossing-point where we become aware of those powerful elements of our lives which we cannot consciously control or even satisfactorily define. This suggests, rightly, that there is a profoundly religious aspect to his response to the world and therefore in his poetry, though he is skeptical of attempts to label his poetry as "religious" for the label may well hide implications he would not accept. Second, we find a steady movement away from the impersonality of the early poetry, a greater willingness to be explicit about his own response to the situations which give rise to the poems. Since the late 1960s his poetry has shown an increasing concern for a certain kind of "truth-telling," which in shorthand could perhaps best be described as a faithfulness to his own verifiable experience. Both of these trends have been amply documented and discussed in Kjell Espmark's study of Tranströmer, published in 1983.

Tranströmer's work is represented in this book rather differently than that of the other three poets: since both a substantial *Selected Poems* and a *Complete Poems* were published in English in 1987 the poems here come from his recent collections *För levande och döda / For Living and Dead* (1989).

Robin Fulton

b. Scotland 1937. *Selected Poems 1963-1978* (Macdonald, Edinburgh, 1980) gathers work from several volumes. Edited the quarterly *Lines Review* from 1967 to 1976 and the associated *Lines Review Editions*; also published *Contemporary Scottish Poets: Individuals and Contexts* (Macdonald, Edinburgh, 1974). Held Writer's Fellowship at Edinburgh University 1969-1971. Has edited Iain Crichton Smith's *Selected Poems 1955-1980* (Macdonald, Edinburgh, 1981). Robert Garioch's *Complete Poetical Works* (Macdonald, Edinburgh, 1983) and *A Garioch Miscellany* (Macdonald, Edinburgh, 1986). His latest collection of poems is *Fields of Focus* (Anvil Press, London, 1982) and *Coming Down to Earth and Spring is Soon* (Oasis / Shearsman, London, 1990).

Swedish writers translated include Werner Aspenström, Stig Dagerman, Gunnar Ekelöf, Kjell Espmark, Lars Gustafsson, Gunnar Harding, Pär Lagerkvist, Östen Sjöstrand, Tomas Tranströmer. For Swedish translations given the Artur Lundkvist award for 1977 and the Swedish Academy award for 1978.

Most recent translation: Olave Hauge's *Don't Give Me the Whole Truth* and other poems (from Norwegian) (Anvil Press, London, 1985); Kjell Espmark, *Bela Bartok against the Third Reich and other poems* (Oasis / Shearsman, London, 1985); Tomas Tranströmer, *Collected Poems* (Bloodaxe Books, Newcastle, 1981).